CANADA

A. Susan Williams
With photographs by Michael Dent

Our Country

Australia
Canada
China
France
India
Italy
Japan
New Zealand
Spain
The United Kingdom
The United States
West Germany

Cover *The fishing village of Stonehurst, Nova Scotia.*

Editor: Joanne Jessop
Designer: Ross George

First published in 1990 by
Wayland (Publishers) Limited
61 Western Road, Hove
East Sussex, BN3 1JD, England

© Copyright 1990 Wayland (Publishers) Limited

British Library Cataloguing in Publication Data
Williams, A. Susan
  Canada.
  1. Canada
  I. Title II. Dent, Michael III. Series
  971.06

  ISBN 1–85210–948–3

Typeset by Nicola Taylor, Wayland.
Printed in Italy by Rotolito Lombardo S.p.A.
Bound in France by A.G.M.

All words printed in **bold** are explained in the glossary on page 30.

Contents

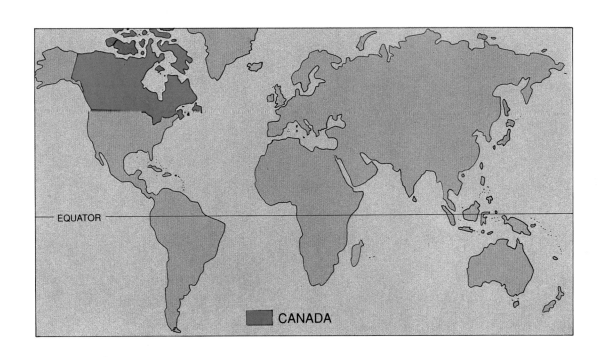

EQUATOR

CANADA

We live in Canada

A pulp and paper mill in British Columbia. There are many rivers and mountains in this province.

Canada is the second largest country in the world. It stretches over the top half of North America and has six different time zones. While Canadians in the **province** of Newfoundland are eating lunch, others in the Yukon are getting up to start the day!

The first Canadians were the **Indians** and the **Inuit**, who are sometimes called Eskimos. The first **settlers** from Britain and France arrived in Canada about 400 years ago. Since then, people from all over the world have come to join the Canadian family. Some live in the two **territories** in the frozen Arctic, but most live in the ten provinces further south. In this book, twelve children in different parts of Canada talk about their lives.

MICHELLE
'I want to be an artist.'

ELLA
'I am an Inuk from northern Quebec.'

DAVID
'I like to play hockey.'

RAYMOND
'My family moved to Canada from Hong Kong.'

DEBBIE
'I live near Edmonton, Alberta.'

KRISTY
'I speak Ukrainian and English.'

ERIN
'I live on a farm in Ontario.'

CARA
'I speak both French and English.'

MELISSA
'My father is a fisher-man.'

TORRY
'I live on a farm in Saskatchewan.'

ADRIANO
'My family runs a restaurant.'

LYDIA
'I am a French-speaking Canadian.'

5

The weather

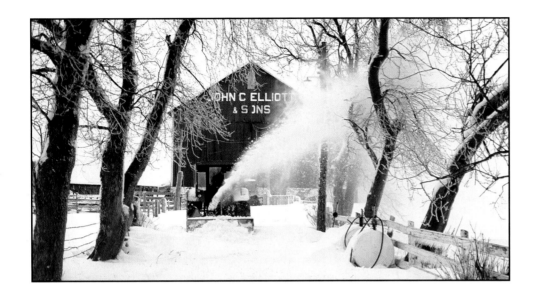

Snow blowers like this one clear the roads after a heavy snowfall.

Some parts of Canada are bitterly cold in winter. Children need to wear thick boots, gloves and woolly hats when they are outdoors. They spend a lot of time dressing and undressing! In the far north, there are no trees because the earth is frozen and blanketed with snow for much of the year. No wonder the Inuit have nearly a hundred different words for snow!

The warmth of spring melts the snow. In Montreal, a city built round a small mountain, the melted snow flows down the mountain into the St Lawrence River. Spring is followed by summer, which can be as hot as the winter is cold. The autumn, which is called 'fall' in Canada, changes the colour of many leaves into lovely shades of orange and brown. The leaves of maple trees turn red and gold. There is a red maple leaf on the Canadian flag.

'I like the fall weather when the leaves change to yellow and orange.'

'My name is Kristy and I live in Manitoba. We have very cold winters and very hot summers. I like the fall weather best. Here I am with my mother, walking in the park near our house. The leaves have changed colour and are beginning to fall from the trees.'

'I play outdoors whenever I can, in summer and in winter.'

'My name is Ella and I live in northern Quebec. The snow comes in October and lasts until May. But I don't mind the cold weather because my sister and I can go skating on the frozen lakes and sledding on my *kamutik* (sledge). In the summer when the weather is warmer and the ice melts, we go for boat rides on the lakes.'

Products of the land

Nature has been generous to Canada. There are forests stretching across the **continent** that provide paper and wood. In the provinces of Quebec and British Columbia, the great quantities of flowing water are used to make electricity. In Alberta there is oil. Valuable **minerals** such as iron ore and nickel are mined in several regions. Fish are caught in the oceans on either side of the country and in its thousands of rivers and lakes.

The **prairie** provinces of Manitoba, Saskatchewan and Alberta, which lie to the

A farm growing wheat in the prairies of Saskatchewan.

'My dad is a fisherman.'

'I am Melissa and I live in Nova Scotia. Our house is beside the sea, and at the bottom of our **backyard** is a jetty where my dad keeps his fishing boat. When he comes back from a day's fishing, I help him to clean the fish and pack them in ice in a big tank. Sometimes I go out in the fishing boat with him.'

'My family runs a farm.'

'My name is Erin and I live on a farm in Ontario. On the farm we breed cattle and grow hay and grain. Some of this is used to feed the cattle; the rest is sold to other farmers. Here I am with one of the bulls. This bull is very friendly and lets me pet him.'

east of the Rocky Mountains, are often described as a 'breadbasket'! This is because so much grain is grown on the fertile prairies. Farmers on the prairies also raise cattle for beef. Quebec produces much of the world's supply of **maple syrup**.

Working in Canada

Many jobs in Canada depend on the forests. **Lumberjacks** fell the trees and send the logs down the rivers. The wood is then cut up in sawmills and made into pulp, paper and plywood. People also work in mines, oil refineries, steel mills and factories.

Canadians serve their **community** in many ways. Some help other people by working as nurses, doctors, secretaries, cleaners, cooks or bus drivers. Others work for the government of their province. If they work for the government of Canada, they might live in Ottawa, the nation's **capital** city. Some children dream of joining the Royal Canadian Mounted Police when they

Moving logs is one of the many jobs to be done in the forests.

'My family runs an Italian restaurant.'

'My name is Adriano and I live in Toronto. My father came to Canada from Italy 25 years ago. He and my mother now own a restaurant. They work very hard, waiting on tables every lunchtime and evening. Here I am in the restaurant learning how a pizza is made.'

'We live on a wheat farm. Dad spends part of his time farming and he also works on oil wells.'

'I am Torry and I live in Saskatchewan. We live on a big wheat farm, and my family also runs a business repairing oil wells. There are lots of oil wells in this part of Canada, so there are lots of calls from people who need to have their oil wells repaired.'

grow up. Mounties are famous throughout the world for their brown hats, scarlet tunics and horses. Today, though, most of them ride in cars, not on horses!

Schools

Most Canadian children start school at the age of five or six. They usually spend their first year in a kindergarten class, which is the first stage of elementary school. In most provinces, children finish elementary school at age twelve and then go to high school. The school day starts in early morning and ends in mid-afternoon. At most schools, boys and girls study together and they do not have to wear a uniform.

Schools in Quebec use French, which is the language spoken by most people in that province. In the English-speaking provinces, the language used at school is

Girls and boys learning together at school.

usually English. In the province of Manitoba, the home of many Ukrainians, some classes are given in the language of the Ukraine. In the north, schools use Inuktitut, the language of the Inuit.

'My school teaches mainly arts such as painting and music.'

'My name is Lydia and I live in Montreal. I speak French at home and at school. My school is a special school that teaches mainly arts such as painting, sculpture, music and dancing, although we study other subjects as well. Here I am showing my father the seedlings I am growing for my science class.'

'I am in grade three and my favourite subject is maths.'

'I am Raymond and this is my classroom at school. I came to this school last year when my family moved to Vancouver from Hong Kong. I have made lots of new friends at my school.'

Religion

These totem poles in western Canada have a religious meaning for the Indians who made them.

Roman Catholics make up the largest religious group in Canada. Half of them live in the province of Quebec. **Protestants** are the second largest religious group in the country. There are also many other religions, as you would expect in a country with people from so many different parts of the world. A growing number of people do not have a religious faith.

When European settlers first arrived in Canada, they tried to stop the Indians and the Inuit from believing in spirits. They wanted them to become Christians instead. But today, everyone is able to follow his or her own beliefs, living side by side in peace.

14

'At Easter we decorate eggs in the traditional Ukrainian style.'

'I am Kristy and here I am with a basket of Ukrainian eggs. It is a Ukrainian tradition to paint designs on eggs at Easter time. Many people who first settled in this part of Canada came from the Ukraine. There are two Ukrainian churches in our town that were built with big domes on top.'

'My family belongs to the United Church of Canada.'

'I am Erin, and my family goes to church every Sunday morning. My sister and I go to Sunday School before the main church service. I like singing, and next year I want to be in the church choir.'

During the spring, for example, Christians observe Easter, the Chinese remember the dead during the festival of *Ching Ming*, and Jews celebrate Passover.

Holidays and festivals

On the first of July in 1867, the separate regions of Canada joined together to become one nation. This birthday is celebrated each year in every province and territory. There are fireworks on Parliament Hill in Ottawa and parades all over the country. Another special day shared by all Canadians is Thanksgiving Day, which is in the autumn. Families eat a turkey dinner and give thanks for their food.

Each province and territory holds special festivals of its own. On Discovery Day in the Yukon, raft races on the Klondike River celebrate the discovery of gold a hundred years ago. In Quebec City, there is a Winter Carnival that lasts for eleven days. There are parades, ice-sculpture contests and a

Mounties on parade at the Calgary Stampede.

canoe race on the frozen St Lawrence River. The Calgary Stampede in Alberta is the world's largest **rodeo**, when men dress up as cowboys and round up cattle.

'On my birthday I had a party and a special birthday cake.'

'My name is Melissa and this is my birthday party. I got lots of nice presents. There were eight candles on my birthday cake because I am eight years old. I made a wish when I blew out the candles. I hope it comes true.'

'For Hallowe'en I like to make a jack-o'-lantern.'

'My name is Cara and I live in Ottawa. Here I am making a jack-o'-lantern by cutting a face into a pumpkin. When I have finished, I will put a small candle inside the pumpkin to light up its face. The jack-o'-lantern sits in our window on Hallowe'en to greet the children who come trick-or-treating to our house.'

Homes

The Indian peoples of the prairies used to live in homes called **teepees**. They were made of poles covered with stretched buffalo skin. The Inuit lived in **igloos**, small houses made of snow blocks. The earliest settlers built log cabins. Today, most people live in modern homes that are centrally heated.

Few people live in the north, because it is so cold. Most Canadians live in the south, within a few hours' drive from the USA border. Some families live in the countryside, but most people live in towns or cities. People in large cities, such as Toronto, Montreal and Vancouver, often live

In suburbs like this, each house has its own garden.

'We live in a big house made of wood.'

'My name is David and I live in New Brunswick. Here I am sitting on the lawn in front of our house. Like many houses in Canada, ours is made of wood. We have a wood-burning furnace to heat the house in winter. There is lots of room to play inside our house and a big yard.'

'We have a big backyard to play in.'

'I am Raymond. My sister and I like to play in our backyard. We are very lucky to have so much space for playing outside. All the houses in our neighbourhood have big backyards. We often invite other children living in our street to come and play on our swings.'

in **apartment** buildings. They can be easily heated in winter and cooled in summer. Many families live in houses in the **suburbs** of cities.

Sports and pastimes

Many activities, such as reading and computer games, can be enjoyed all the year round. Canadian children have a wide choice of television programmes because they can get American as well as Canadian channels on television. In Quebec, there are both French and English channels.

Outdoor fun depends on the weather. In the winter, children make snowmen, ride **toboggans**, ski and ice skate. The Rideau Canal in Ottawa becomes the largest outdoor skating rink in the world! In the summer, children can enjoy sports such as swimming and baseball. In the holidays, they might visit other parts of their country. The Rocky Mountains in British Columbia

Skiing is a winter sport enjoyed by many Canadian children.

'I am goalie for our hockey team.'

'My name is David and I play goalie for our hockey team. Hockey is my favourite sport. I am lucky because our town has a hockey arena. The hockey season lasts from November to April. In the summer I like to play baseball.'

'Drawing and painting are what I like to do most of all.'

'My name is Michelle and I live on an Ojibwa Indian **Reserve** in Ontario. Here I am with my sister and one of my paintings. I love to paint and draw. I want to be an artist when I grow up.'

and Niagara Falls in Ontario are favourite attractions. Camping in national parks is a perfect way to see the wilderness – you might see moose, bears and beavers. If you are camping by the sea, you might even see seals or whales plunging through the waves.

Food

Stopping for a snack on a hot summer day.

Canadians eat lots of different foods. For instance, children in an Italian community might eat Italian food at home but Canadian food at school. A packed lunch for school might be a carton of apple juice and a sandwich filled with peanut butter and jam. A school dinner might be a hamburger with french fries (the Canadian word for chips) and a salad.

Each region of Canada has its own favourite meals. On the prairies, it is a treat to barbecue a whole calf in a pit. Children in Quebec go to 'sugaring-off' parties in the spring. Maple trees are **tapped** to produce sap, which becomes a delicious toffee when it has been cooked and then thrown on to the snow. People in Saskatchewan enjoy a corn roast, when they eat corn on the cob that has been roasted in the glowing coals of a bonfire.

'Pizza is my favourite food.'

'I am Adriano. My brothers and I are having a pizza at our family's restaurant. We often come here for a pizza after school when the restaurant is closed. Pizza is my favouite food, but I also like hamburgers and french fries.'

'I always enjoy a spaghetti dinner.'

'My name is Debbie and I live in Alberta. Here I am enjoying a spaghetti dinner. This is my favourite meal, but I also enjoy baked potatoes, salads and raw vegetables with cheese dip. For dessert, I love to have ice-cream and apple pie.'

Shopping

Most neighbourhoods have a supermarket nearby. Although these are convenient, many people like to visit their local shops as well. In Vancouver's Chinatown, for example, there are shops selling delicious foods for Chinese meals. Children like to spend their pocket money on comics, chewing gum and candy, which is the Canadian word for sweets.

Shopping can be unpleasant when it is very cold. This problem has been solved by indoor shopping **malls**, which are heated in the winter and air-conditioned in the summer. They provide all sorts of shops and parking for cars, so that no one has to step

Vancouver's Chinatown has lots of interesting shops.

'Outdoor markets are fun.'

'I am Cara and here I am shopping with my Grandad. We usually shop for food at a supermarket, but an outdoor market is a lot more fun. There are many stalls selling different types of food. Grandad and I are choosing some fresh vegetables. My favourite stall is the one that sells cakes and cookies.'

'I help my Mom shop at the supermarket.'

'I am Torry and I like getting a ride in Mom's shopping cart. Every week we go to the supermarket. We buy all the food we will need for the week. I enjoy helping Mom with the shopping.'

outside. One of the largest shopping malls in the world is the West Edmonton Mall in Edmonton, Alberta. It has eight hundred stores, restaurants, an aquarium with dolphins and sharks, a skating rink, and thirty-four cinemas!

Transport

You can drive through the Rocky Mountains on the Trans-Canada Highway.

In the past, the Inuit used sledges pulled by dogs to cross snowy distances. They now use **snowmobiles**, fuelled by petrol. Aeroplanes are the quickest way of reaching **isolated** communities.

Further south, Indians and early **traders** used to get about on horses, on snowshoes and in canoes. Today, there are quicker ways of travelling – trains, aeroplanes, boats, buses and cars. Roads link most areas of Canada together. The Trans-Canada Highway, which stretches all the way from the Atlantic coast to the Pacific coast, is the longest road in the world. In the winter, salt and sand are sprinkled on

26

roads to stop cars from skidding on the ice.

There is good public transport in Canada. The city of Toronto, for example, has underground trains, electric streetcars and buses. To get to school, children walk, ride bikes, or are driven in cars or school buses.

'I go to school on the school bus.'

'I am Debbie and every morning the school bus comes to our house to take us to school in town. In winter, when there is a heavy snowfall, the bus cannot get to our house until the snowploughs have cleared the snow from the roads. When this happens, we are sometimes late for school.'

'I love to go on boat rides.'

'I am Melissa and here I am in our boat with my brothers. We live by the sea, and I love to go on boat rides. Sometimes we use the boat to visit our neighbours, but mostly we use it just to have fun.'

Let's discuss Canada

English-speaking Canadians speak the same language as we do, using their own accent. But some of their words are different. Their word for chips, for example, is french fries, and their word for crisps is chips! Do you know any other Canadian words that are different?

This book has told you a little about Canada and the lives of some Canadian children. Which one do you have most in

Facts

Population: 26,000,000
Capital: Ottawa
Language: French and English
Money: Canadian dollar
Religion: Mainly Roman Catholic and Protestant

The harbour at Vancouver, on Canada's western coast.

common with? Why? Is it because you both live in the same sort of place – in a town or on a farm, for example? Or is it because you have similar interests?

Which part of Canada would you most like to visit? Why? Which season would you prefer? If you wanted to describe your life to a child in Canada, what would you say?

Canada is a country of snow and ice in the winter.

Glossary

Apartment The Canadian word for a flat; a group of rooms that is a home.

Backyard The word Canadians use to describe their garden.

Capital The city that is the seat of a nation's government.

Community A group of people living in one place together, or having something else in common with each other.

Continent One of the seven largest land masses of the earth, such as North America.

Igloo A house built of blocks of snow used by the Inuit.

Indian The name the European settlers called the native people they found living in North America, such as the Iroquois and the Cree.

Inuit The word used by the people living in the north of Canada to describe themselves. In their language, Inuit means people. They are sometimes (inaccurately) called Eskimos.

Isolated Lonely, or cut off from other people.

Lumberjack A person who cuts down trees.

Mall An indoor shopping centre.

Maple syrup A syrup that is made from the sap of the sugar maple tree, which grows in North America.

Minerals Substances such as coal and iron that can be dug out of the ground. Minerals are used in industry.

Prairie A large, flat and treeless area, stretching for huge distances across southern Canada and central USA.

Protestants Members of the Protestant Church, a branch of Christianity.

Province In Canada, one of the ten regions that – together with two Territories – make up the nation.

Reserve An area of land that has been set aside for use by Indians. Many Canadian Indians live on reserves.

Rodeo An exhibition of the skills of cowboys, such as the rounding up of cattle.

Roman Catholics Members of the Roman Catholic Church, headed by the Pope.

Settlers People who go to live in a new country.

Snowmobile A motor vehicle that travels over snow.

Suburb The area surrounding a city centre.

Tapping Drawing off sap (fluid) from a tree.

Teepee A tent made of poles covered with stretched buffalo skin. The Indians of the North

American priaries originally lived in teepees.

Territory In Canada, one of the two regions in the North that – together with ten Provinces – make up the nation.

Toboggan A sledge with boards curved around at the front end.

Traders People who buy or sell goods. The early European traders in Canada traded mainly in furs.

Books to read

Canada by Jack Brickenden (Wayland, 1987)

Canada a project by Clifford Education (Macmillan, 1988)

Canada Is My Country by B. and C. Moon (Wayland, 1985)

Canadian Family by Nancy D. McKenna (A & C Black, 1988)

Inuit by Ann Smith (Wayland, 1989)

Morning Sun and the Lost Girl by Neil and Ting Morris (Hodder & Stoughton Children's Books, 1984)

They Sought A New World: The Story of European Immigrants to North America by William Kurelek (Tundra Books, 1985)

The Time of the Indian by Kenneth Ulyatt (Kestrel Books, 1975)

Picture acknowledgements

The publishers would like to thank the following for supplying pictures: Bryan & Cherry Alexander *cover inset*, 7; Wayland Picture Library 8, Zefa 8, 16. All other photographs by Michael Dent. The map on page 5 was supplied by Jenny Hughes.

Index